Ray,

Warmest wishes to you and your family for a happy and safe holiday season,

Bob Lutz

12/88

Landscapes of America

SECOND SERIES

CLB 1609
© 1987 Illustrations and text: Colour Library Books Ltd.,
   Guildford, Surrey, England.
Text filmsetting by Acesetters Ltd., Richmond, Surrey, England.
All rights reserved.
1987 edition published by Crescent Books, distributed by Crown Publishers, Inc.
Printed and bound in Barcelona. Spain by Cronion, S.A.
ISBN 0 517 61393 X
h g f e d c b a
Dep. Leg. B-996-87

Landscapes of America

SECOND SERIES

Text by

Bill Harris

CRESCENT BOOKS
NEW YORK

On a crisp day in 1977, a big jet from Europe touched down at the airport in Bangor, Maine. Erwin Kreuz, a brewery worker from West Germany, strolled into the terminal building for a sample of the local beer, which he found acceptable; then he set out to see the sights.

Maine is spectacular in October. The forests are scarlet, yellow and orange, the air is crystal clear, and though winter is on the way, Indian summer is still there. Mr. Kreuz had obviously picked a perfect time to visit.

He drank it in for three days. But all the while, he had a strange feeling that something was wrong. Something was. He thought he was in San Francisco. There are no cable cars in Bangor, no Golden Gate, no Chinatown, no Fisherman's Wharf, no Nob Hill. They're all 3,000 miles away!

The story has a happy ending though. They treated him like a king in Maine for a week, then packed him off to the West Coast where the party went on for another week.

His adventure is almost the story of America. Back in 1492, Christopher Columbus discovered it, but he was so sure he was someplace else, he named the natives "Indians." Columbus was out to prove the world was round, and he was certain he could reach the exotic East by sailing west, so it's obvious he thought he was in India. When he realized he wasn't, he moved on.

About 500 years before him, Norsemen led by Leif Ericson apparently stumbled on North America. They called it "Vinland The Good," but didn't think it was good enough either to stay or even make a record of their visit.

There are stories that Swedes and Norwegians came to America from Greenland in the 13th century. And still more that say America was really discovered by the Irish, or the Welsh, or the Chinese, or the Phoenicians. But through it all, none of them seems to have known what they discovered. And none of them cared.

Once it had been discovered, however, people came to explore it. And in almost every case, what they were really looking for was a way *around* it, or even *through* it.

Columbus never knew he had discovered a whole new continent, but he found out enough about it to know that it was rich in gold and silver; and to the Spanish who financed his expedition, that was a whole lot better than spices from the Orient or some half-baked theory about the shape of the world. Within 20 years they were exporting a million dollars a year in gold and silver from America, and that encouraged them to look around for more.

In the process they established colonies, including St. Augustine on the Florida peninsula in 1565. It was the first permanent European settlement in the United States. So permanent, it's still there.

Meanwhile, watching Spain's wealth growing encouraged others to explore this new world. French explorers claimed all the territory from the Carolinas north to the St. Lawrence River and settled in Nova Scotia, Florida and South Carolina.

The English got into the act, too. But they found it more fun to raid the Spanish treasure ships than to build towns and farms. One of the pirates, Sir Walter Raleigh, used his Spanish treasure to start a colony in Virginia. Though his original colony ultimately failed, it did succeed in introducing tobacco to the world and helped the British realize there was, perhaps, more to America that gold and silver.

In the first half of the 17th century Europeans began arriving and settling down. The English set up shop in Jamestown, Virginia, in 1607. A year later the French arrived in Quebec. Twenty years later, the Dutch founded Nieuw Amsterdam, and ten years after that the Swedes established a colony in Delaware. The Dutch eased them out rather quickly; then the British moved the Dutch out of their colony and renamed it New York.

While all this was going on, the French were pushing inland toward the Great Lakes and down the Mississippi to the Gulf of Mexico. The stage was set for war.

There were four wars in all, beginning with one called "King William's War," and ending with one called "The Seven Years War." Oddly enough, none was fought in America, but America was what they were all about. When they were over, France had lost claim to her American colonies, and England and Spain divided up the country between them. Under the treaty, Spain got all the territory west of the Mississippi and England claimed everything to the east.

The Spaniards thought they had made a good deal. They had found great riches among the Aztecs and Incas in Mexico and South America, and the Indians told them there were "Seven Cities of Gold" to the north. Indeed, a Spanish priest in search of heathens to convert had reported seeing one of them somewhere near where the Arizona-New Mexico border is today. They had been exploring the territory for a century, going as far north as Kansas, as far west as California. They didn't find the "Seven Cities of Gold" – no one ever has – but they were fairly certain they weren't east of the Mississippi.

The British were slow starters in colonizing America, but ultimately their colonies were the most successful. In 1620, just a few years after the founding of the Virginia colony, a group of religious dissenters arrived in Cape Cod Bay, Massachusetts. As Puritans, life under James I in England had been less than joyous, even to these people who considered "joy" a four-letter word. With the King's blessing 101 of them, and a ship's crew of 48, had set off to escape persecution and to find a new life in the New World.

Their ship, of course, was the "Mayflower;" their colony, Plymouth, and they are remembered today as "Pilgrims." They were Englishmen first, travelling with the permission of the Crown and at the expense of The London Company, who owned the settlements in Virginia.

Some say they were off course, some say it was a careful plan; but the fact is, they landed far north of the Virginia colony outside the jurisdiction of The London Company. This left them free to make their own rules, and before leaving the ship they drew up a document that became the law of their colony. Basically, it bound them together voluntarily to obey the rule of the majority. It was an almost revolutionary idea in 1620, and it became the first step toward another, bigger, revolutionary idea, the United States Constitution.

Life was far from easy for the colonists on Cape Cod Bay, but they managed to survive in spite of it. Within 20 years, they had a thriving colony of hard-working souls. A decade later, they had absorbed more than 20,000 in the biggest mass migration England has ever seen. To make room for the newcomers, they started some new towns with such names as Cambridge, Charlestown, Gloucester and Boston.

As often happens when oppressed people look for freedom, the Massachusetts settlers didn't give much freedom to people who didn't agree with them. It wasn't long before they had dissenters among themselves, who went down the Cape to start a colony of their own, which they called Rhode Island.

The soil in Massachusetts was poor for farming, so another group set out further south and settled down in Connecticut, which made the Dutch in Nieuw Amsterdam very nervous indeed. More of them went up to the southern coast of Maine, which had already been settled by the French, and still more moved west into New Hampshire.

The Indians had been friendly, even helpful, to the colonists, but all this expansion was too much. The Puritans didn't believe in buying territory from the natives; they just marched in and took it. The tribes in Connecticut didn't think that was right, and so they rebelled by attacking the settlements, In retaliation, a force went out from Massachusetts and wiped out an entire tribe, destroying their villages and capturing survivors to sell as slaves in the West Indies. That solved their immediate problem, but gave them a much bigger one in return. And so to protect themselves from the hostile savages, the colonists bound themselves together in a confederation they called "New England."

Meanwhile, people were pouring into the New World from old England. The King was giving away huge tracts of land to both his creditors and his old friends. One of those friends, Sir George Calvert, had visited Virginia and liked it very much. But he wasn't allowed to stay because he was a Roman Catholic. The King fixed that by giving him land north of Virginia. Calvert died soon after, and the grant went to his son, the second Lord Baltimore, who named the estate "Maryland," and established it as a colony for English Catholics.

The southern and middle colonies were run almost like feudal estates. The grants decreed that any laws passed should not violate English law and should have the consent of the people. But the landowners were free to give or sell land to settlers on whatever terms they decided. Baltimore's terms were possibly the most feudal in the entire British Empire, and his colony was slow to grow. He also faced unreasonable anti-Catholicism, and finally the third Lord Baltimore was forced to convert to the Anglican Church to keep control of his grandfather's grant.

Not all the settlers in the English colonies came from England. By the time King Charles II repaid some favors by giving the Carolinas to eight of his cronies, not many Englishmen were eager to leave home. But Barbados and the other British West Indies islands had become very crowded, and some of the planters there were more than happy to migrate north and west. They brought along an institution that would become an American tradition for the next 200 years: slavery.

Once the English had convinced the Dutch that New Netherland was not a healthy place to live, the King gave the territory to his brother, the Duke of York, who in turn gave it his name. He gave the southern part of his grant to two of his friends, who called it "New Jersey."

They, in turn, sold part of their land to a group of Quakers, one of whom was William Penn. The land didn't have access to the ocean, so Penn approached the Duke of York, who had taken over a territory to the south on the mistaken assumption that it was part of his grant. Penn bought it from him and established a colony called "Delaware."

William Penn's father had been a close friend to, and creditor of, the King. Penn inherited the friendship and the unpaid debt, for which he accepted an American land grant. He set up a colony called "Pennsylvania," dedicated to complete religious freedom. Though intended as a refuge for Quakers, he welcomed anyone, and as a result, his was the fastest-growing colony America had yet seen. The Quakers came in huge numbers, along with Mennonites, Baptists, Jews and others. They came from Wales and Scotland and Ireland, from Sweden and from Germany. And they all agreed that they liked what they found there. Even the natives were friendly. Penn was fair-minded to a fault, and made it a point to pay the Indians for their land. He also made treaties that were fair to both sides and made sure that they were backed up. The result was that Pennsylvania farmers, who didn't own guns, lived in complete peace with the Indians, while settlers all around them lived in terror of the "savages."

It was more that 50 years later that the last of the major English colonies was established, when James Oglethorpe set up Georgia as a haven for people from the debtors' prisons in England.

Over the following 40 years, cities grew, farmers and trappers began moving further west and immigrants kept pouring in from all over Europe. By 1760, the population had reached 1,700,000, the country was prosperous and the cities cosmopolitan. A whole continent stretched out to the west waiting to be conquered. But first, the British had to be overcome.

It started quietly, of course. Most wars do. Word had gone out that the British were going to Lexington in Massachusetts to arrest a pair of rebels named Sam Adams and John Hancock. About 70 patriots, calling themselves "Minutemen," assembled on the village green to take a stand against them. And there, on April 19, 1775, a pistol shot rang out, followed by a volley of rifle fire from the British Redcoats. Within a month, Great Britain was at war with her American colonies. The war would last until 1781, when General George Washington, with the help of the French Marquis de Lafayette, defeated the British forces at Yorktown in Virginia. As the British marched away, their band played an old march, "The World Turned Upside Down." And for them it had.

For the first time, the American stars and stripes fluttered over a free and independent nation.

That flag had 13 stars; today it has 50. At the time the peace treaty that officially ended the war was signed, the United States covered 800,000 square miles from Maine to Georgia and from the Atlantic to the Mississippi. Today it covers more than 3,600,000. There were about 3 million Americans then. Today the population has grown to more than 230 million.

What is a typical American? There is really no such thing, but combining census statistics, the typical American family would seem to live in a metropolitan suburb at about the point where Wyoming, Montana and South Dakota come together. Since there are no big cities anywhere near there, one can't help being cynical about statistical evidence. But to press on... the typical American family, according to the census, owns its own home, which is worth about $17,000 (in a metropolitan suburb!). The family is about 90 percent white, but speaks a little Spanish, looks slightly Oriental and has ancestors who were pure American Indians. The man of the house is 44 years old and he's married to a woman who admits to 41. They have 2.35 children, whom they support on an income of $9,867. That makes them affluent enough to own one and a quarter automobiles.

And so on. Every American family appears to own three radios, and more Americans own a TV set than have a bathtub or a shower in their house. They're religious, too. Only about 5 percent say they have no religion at all. And of the rest, 66 percent are Protestant, 26 percent are Catholic and 3 percent are Jewish. The other 5 percent are divided among just about every religion known to mankind.

People are fond of calling America a "melting pot." But in the melting process, most of the people who migrated to the United States from other countries brought a little of the old country with them. It's as common for one American to ask another what nationality he is as to ask about his astrological sign. And some of the answers are amazing. "I'm English-Irish-German and Swedish," one might say. Or the answer might be more simply, "I'm an Italian-American." During political campaigns, it's as common to hear calls for an end to such "hyphenated Americanism" as it is to hear pleas that "no American should go to bed hungry." And with rhetoric like that, it's no wonder only about half the eligible voters ever go to the polls!

But the fact is, most Americans enjoy the sense of community that comes from sharing their roots. And while many Americans do go to bed hungry, an overwhelming percentage of them are on diets, and the average family in the United States spends more on food alone than the total annual income of the average Greek family.

It's a nation of movers. Some 20 percent look for greener pastures every year, and sometimes the moving almost amounts to a mass migration. In the last 50 years, huge numbers have moved from the South to the North and thousands more have gone the other way. Farm workers have moved to the cities; city folks have moved to the suburbs, and California doesn't ever seem to stop growing.

But the more they move, the more the population centers seem to stay the same. Only about 1.5 percent of the land in the United States is taken up by cities and towns, and more than half the people live close enough to have a Sunday picnic on the shores of the Atlantic or Pacific Oceans, the Gulf of Mexico or one of the Great Lakes. It's still very much a country of wide open spaces, and even though only about a quarter of all native-born Americans still live in the state in which they were born, more than a quarter of the total population lives along the Atlantic Coast, about the same percentage that lived there a century ago.

But almost from the beginning, the pull was from the West. After the Revolution, the Spanish still controlled Florida and the land west of the Mississippi. The British had never bothered to leave Ohio, and just about everything west of the original 13 colonies was wilderness occupied by trappers and traders, Indians and a few farmers. A generation later, the United States had bought "Louisiana," an area that began at

the Mississippi, went past Texas, and stretched west into present-day Montana and Wyoming. It doubled the size of the country and opened vast opportunities for immigrants.

People began taking advantage of the opportunity in the 1820s, when German and Irish immigrants arrived in big numbers, eager for a new life and willing to take a chance on the wild frontier. People who had been born in places like Connecticut and Maryland joined them, lured by the promise of cheap land. Farmers from the already soil-exhausted South picked up stakes and went along, too. Others went in search of adventure, some went to escape debt. But most went West because it was there. It gave them a chance to start a new life, something Americans are still doing more than 150 years later.

By the time the migration to the West gained real impetus, there were passable roads across the Appalachian Mountains. The migrants went in Conestoga wagons, in pack trains and in fancy stage coaches. Once across the mountains, the Ohio River took them into Tennessee and Kentucky... all the way to the Mississippi, in fact, and from there up to the Great Lakes, down to the Gulf of Mexico and across into Missouri and Arkansas.

Their new homes needed to be established in hostile wilderness, populated by Indians who didn't much like seeing their homelands turned into farms and by Europeans who egged the savages on. But those who went into Ohio found signs of a very friendly man who made it his mission in life to make their lives pleasanter.

His name was John Chapman. When he died in the 1830s, the Fort Wayne, Indiana, *Sentinel* reported:

"Died in the neighborhood of this city, on Tuesday last, Mr. John Chapman, better known as Johnny Appleseed. The deceased was well-known throughout this region by his eccentricity, and the strange garb he usually wore. He followed the occupation of nursery-man."

Remembering Johnny Appleseed as a "nurseryman" is almost the same as remembering George Washington as a "planter." He wandered through the wilderness for more than 50 years planting apple trees as well as other fruits and medicinal plants he knew would be useful to the settlers who followed him.

He began his wanderings in Pittsburgh, after having planted orchards all the way from Massachusetts to Pennsylvania. Everyone who knew him loved him, even the Indians who were generally hostile to the white men. But even those who loved him most had to agree he cut quite a bizarre figure. They say he wore a coffee sack with holes cut in it for arms, and a stewing kettle passed for a hat. He would appear mysteriously at the door of a settler's cabin to ask for a place to spend the night. When he was welcomed inside, he always refused to sleep anywhere but on the floor, and before the sun rose in the morning, he had vanished as silently as he had appeared.

Once, when the city of Mansfield, Ohio, was being attacked by Indians, Chapman ran 30 miles to the nearest fort and was back again with help in less than 24 hours. Another story about him, which may or may not be true, was that he was seen in the woods playing with a family of bear cubs while their mother watched benignly. He always walked barefoot, even in winter, and could find his way anywhere without a compass.

Deeply religious, he led an utterly selfless life. He didn't own a gun, and couldn't hurt a living thing. A legend about him says he once doused a campfire so mosquitoes wouldn't be burned to death in the flame. He wouldn't eat meat, and would never accept anything from anyone unless he could exchange it for seeds or a small tree.

When Ohio began to get too "crowded" for him, he moved further west into Indiana, where he finally died. For years after, people on the frontier told affectionate stories about this wonderful little man. There were so many stories, in fact, that people who didn't know better began to think there had never been such a person as Johnny Appleseed.

By the time he died, more than a million people had settled in Ohio. Almost 4 million lived west of the Allegheny Mountains, and nine more states, including Illinois, Missouri and Alabama had joined the original 13.

At about the same town, President Monroe decided it was about time to get rid of some of those Indians who stood in the way of expansion. General Andrew Jackson and Indiana's Governor William Henry Harrison, each a future President, had defused the Indian menace on the frontier and a new standing army kept it that way. Now, new treaties dictated that Eastern tribes should move West ahead of the wave of immigrants. The Creeks, Cherokees, Choctaws, Chickasaws and Seminoles were all forced to walk what they called "The Trail of Tears" into what the Government called "Indian Territory."

They called it "progress." It's a thing Americans still believe in with unabashed enthusiasm. No problem is so great that "American ingenuity" can't solve it. America first discovered its courage in these people who moved West in the 19th century. They took civilization into the wilderness and made it work. Long before the century was half over, the country was well on its way, not just to the Pacific Coast, but to a position of importance in the world no country so young had a right to expect.

One of the people who originally explored the land just west of the mountains fired the imagination of would-be frontiersmen and still inspires Americans today. His name was Daniel Boone. He was a Pennsylvanian who moved to North Carolina as a boy and spent most of his life exploring Kentucky.

On his first long trip he was captured and robbed by Indians four times, and after two years of hunting came back empty-handed. But he loved every minute of the adventure, and he became a master of Indian psychology as well as an enthusiastic hunter and explorer. His tales of the wilderness encouraged a North Carolina entrepreneur to buy Kentucky and part of Tennessee from the Cherokee Indians. His stories also got him the job of mapping a road through the territory. Once into the interior, he built a town, which he modestly called "Boonesboro." Not long after, he was taken prisoner by Shawnee Indians determined to capture and destroy the settlement. But he talked them out of it and in the process so charmed them that they adopted him into their tribe, changed his name to "Big Turtle," and treated him as the son of their chief.

But all the while, he was still their prisoner.

It was several months before he escaped and got back to Boonesboro to warn his friends the Indians were coming. When they arrived, the settlers were ready for them, resolved to fight to the death to save their town.

They nearly had to. The Shawnee kept at it for two months, trying every trick in their book to destroy the settlement. But Boone knew their tricks and so none of them worked. Finally, the Indians tried to tunnel under the stockade. Boone dug a trench in their way, but they kept at it. Then a heavy rain made their tunnel collapse and the Indians went home in disgust.

He had saved his home, but Daniel Boone was never a homebody. Leaving the great "Wilderness Road" as a permanent monument, he set out to explore even more of the country. At 65, when people today think of retiring, he joined the Lewis and Clark expedition up the Missouri River and into the Oregon Territory.

He opened the way for people as tough as himself. Men and women with large families of children built cabins in the middle of the woods. They generally cleared 40 acres or so by stripping the bark from the trees so they would die. Once dead, it was a simple matter to burn away the trunks and dig out the stumps. They burned the tall grass away so new grass would feed their cattle, and planted grain on the land they had cleared. Women looked after the children, of course, when they weren't cooking, churning, hoeing, spinning, chopping wood or carrying water.

Not everyone lived in the wilderness, though. Great cities were being established, too. Cincinnati, Pittsburgh and Detroit were all lusty and thriving at the beginning of the 19th century, and in a 1795 treaty, the Indians had turned over "a piece of land six miles square at the mouth of the Chickago River, emptying into the southwest end of Lake Michigan, where a fort formerly stood." In 1803 a new fort was built there to stand guard over the gateway to the Northwest Territory. Some French traders, holdovers from the days when this was French territory, lived across the river.

The fort was destroyed in the war of 1812, and yet another was built after the war was over. It was a center for the fur trade until the market dropped, and was again reborn as the City of Chicago when a canal was dug over the old portage route the French trappers had used.

New York City has an international flavor that can't be matched by any other city in the world. San Francisco has a classic charm that makes it the favorite of most Americans; Denver has a setting that makes most other cities envious, but no other city is as truly "American" as Chicago, Illinois. New York, Boston and Philadelphia were well into their second century when people began settling down along the lake shore. But this city was different. For the first time,

possibly in the history of the world, builders asked *women* what sort of houses they'd like. The answer was loud and clear. They wanted porches and big bay windows and yards that went around all four sides of the house instead of the attached row houses of other cities. They got what they wanted. It was a neighborly place then and it still is.

Chicago is where modern architecture was born and where it exists at its best. It's the city of Frank Lloyd Wright and Mies van der Rohe and the man who started it all, Louis Sullivan. Sullivan's philosophy was based on the tradition of the early builders who took the trouble to talk with the people who had to use their buildings. He didn't think a bank should look like a fortress or a factory like a tomb. In later years, his ideas would be taken to Europe and sent back as something new. But, as can be seen in the "improvements" in cities like Atlanta and Houston, the switch from "Chicago Style" to "International Style" had a very sterilizing effect on the original idea that "a building is an act."

The good news is that Chicago is alive and well. Anyone on a search for America would do well to begin there. In its early days, once the frontier had pushed that far west, it became the gateway to the Golden West. But the door swung both ways. It also became the gateway to the East and South for the ranchers and farmers from the West, and by the time the Civil War broke out Chicago was already what Carl Sandberg later called it: "Hog butcher for the world."

When the railroads pushed West, Chicago was at the center of the activity. It still has the biggest railroad terminal in the world and the busiest airport, and it's still the gateway to the Golden West.

The territory north of Chicago: Wisconsin, Michigan, Minnesota and all the way west to Oregon, was a land of logging camps in the early days. Instead of burning out the forests as the pioneers to the south and east had done, they were at work providing the raw material to build a country.

The loggers in the Northwest, the keelboatmen on the Mississippi, the farmers and the builders, were all made of tough stuff. There was hard work to be done, and they were the right people for the job. Hard work had been an American tradition right from the start, and they made it look easy.

Another quality Americans have always admired is "rugged individualism." The Yankees in New England respected it as much as their religion, and it went west along with the country.

When Indiana was still an untamed frontier, the territory between the Missouri River and the Spanish missions in California was wild, hostile, unexplored country. It was a perfect setting for the rugged individualists they called "mountain men."

It was all the rage in London and Paris in the 1820s to own soft felt hats made of beaver hair. They were as expensive as they were fashionable, and beaver pelts brought good prices. Trappers, armed with big rifles, pistols, tomahawks and hunting knives ran their lines across the plains and into the Rocky Mountains beyond. In later years, Buffalo Bill made himself the personification of these mountain men, who were the first white men to see the huge herds of buffalo on the plains, the first to ride through the Rockies, the first to fight the Apache and other hostile Indians in the West. They wore big-brimmed hats and fringed leather shirts and pants; their faces were smeared with campfire grease and their hair streamed out behind them as they rode their horses over trails only Indians had ever seen.

They lived their lives in the mountains and on the prairies, slipping back east about once a year to meet traders who went out from St. Louis to meet them and to exchange beaver pelts for whiskey and fresh clothes.

Meanwhile, the Spanish hadn't given up looking for the fabled "Seven Cities of Gold," but by now they had confined their activities to the Southwest from New Mexico and across Texas into California. They had missions and settlements up the California coast from San Diego to San Francisco. And, as if they didn't have enough troubles in the desert peopled by angry Indians, the Russians were coming.

The Czar was as interested as anyone else in Europe in finding a "Northwest Passage" across North America, and he sent an explorer named Vitus Bering to take a look.

Bering explored Alaska and discovered it was rich in otter, a happy little animal whose fur was very highly-prized in China. That lured trappers from Siberia, who ranged down the coast to within about 50 miles of the Spanish settlement at San Francisco.

At the same time, British fur traders moved west across Canada. And Americans, including a New Yorker named John Jacob Astor, set up trading posts at the edge of the Oregon territory. The days of Spanish California were clearly numbered.

Back East, Americans were dreaming a new dream. Until then, the lure had been gold or timber or furs. But the American dream was for the land itself. Many of the immigrants from Europe had come from peasant stock, and the idea of actually owning their own land was almost too good to be true. They came to believe it was their sacred duty to carry civilization west. A New York newspaper told them... "Our manifest destiny is to overspread and to possess the whole of the continent which Providence has given us for the development of the great experiment of liberty and federated self-government."

That was all they needed!

The major trials began at Independence, Missouri, jumping off place for the Santa Fe Trail into the Southwest or the Oregon Trail that headed north towards the Columbia River. It was a boom town in the 1840s, with pioneers arriving with huge families and all their belongings loaded into ox-drawn, canvas-covered wagons. They usually stopped there for a while, buying supplies, hiring a mountain man to guide them and organizing themselves into trains of at least 40 wagons.

They took cattle with them, so they had to wait in Independence until the grass of the prairie was abundant enough to feed the stock. And since they all believed in the code of "rugged individualism," it wasn't easy for them to organize themselves into congenial groups.

Once under way on the Oregon Trail, they found the Kansas and Nebraska countryside beautiful, if ominously quiet and desolate. The boredom was often broken by wild rainstorms that washed out their camps and flooded the streams they had to cross.

The wagons traveled four or more abreast so they could be organized into protective squares if Indians attacked. The men walked with the oxen to keep them moving, the boys kept the cattle from straying and the women sat at the front of the wagon, usually knitting.

The going got rougher when they reached Chimney Rock in Western Nebraska and their wagon wheels began to sink into the sandy soil. They were usually out of firewood by then, and as there were no trees to cut, they cooked over buffalo chip fires. Fort Laramie, in Wyoming, offered them a chance to load fresh supplies, to repair their wagons and to steel themselves for the hard part of the trip: the Rockies.

The route across Wyoming toward Idaho was littered with cast-off furniture, abandoned to make the wagons less burdensome for the starving oxen. It was uphill all the way until they reached a pass that took them through the mountains and over the top to find even more hostile, barren country ahead.

If they were lucky enough to make it before winter, they settled down in Oregon and California. And they never looked back. Yet, oddly, even native Californians today refer to everything on the other side of the Mississippi as "back East."

The Oregon Trail was laid out by the Lewis and Clark expedition; the Santa Fe Trail was the route of mule trains and caravans of ox carts that carried American trade from Independence down into New Mexico. It stretched almost 800 miles across the desert and through Apache country, so it wasn't as popular with the early emigrants until gold fever hit them in 1849 and people started heading west for different reasons.

A third major route to the West began in Palmyra, New York, a small town near the Erie Canal. A man named Joseph Smith was plowing his field there one day when an angel, who said his name was Moroni, introduced him to God and His Son.

"The Book of Mormon," which Smith translated from buried golden tablets to which the angel had directed him, became the basis for a whole new religion. Some people in Palmyra didn't like the idea and they ran Smith and his followers out of town. They had the same experience in Ohio and then in Missouri, but even as they kept moving, Smith's following was growing. They finally settled along the Mississippi in an Illinois town they called Nauvoo. Before long, it was the biggest city in the entire state, with 15,000 residents, and the Mormons thought they were safe at last. But they weren't. Nauvoo was surrounded by "Gentiles," as Smith called non-Mormons, who weren't too neighborly or tolerant of these people who were said to practice polygamy. When Smith ordered a newspaper destroyed because it was critical of him, the Gentiles made their move. They lynched Joseph Smith.

Brigham Young became their leader, and he took on the mission of leading his people to a new land where there were no Gentiles. They sold their houses in Nauvoo and built wagons to make a long trip to the Great Salt Lake, which had been discoved some years before by Western explorers.

A few had oxen to pull their wagons, but most loaded their belongings into hand carts and started the long walk west. By the fall of 1847, some 2,000 of them had reached the "Promised Land," but what they found there was a dry, sun-baked plain. They put themselves completely under the control of their church, and together made the valley bloom. Meanwhile, thousands of converts arrived from the East and from Europe, and a string of settlements sprang up. There were enough of them before long for Brigham Young to announce that they had established an independent nation. He called it "Deseret." The U.S. Government called it the Territory of Utah, but it took 50 years for them to make the idea stick.

Even the Civil War didn't slow down the rush to the West. In the year General Sherman marched through Georgia, some 75,000 people marched in wagon trains along the Oregon Trail. And after the war ended in 1865, freed slaves and war veterans poured across the Mississippi looking for adventure and opportunity. What they found was what they themselves created: the Wild West.

Most of the big cattle spreads were in Texas and Colorado, but the Texas ranchers drove their longhorns as far north as the Dakota Territory to fatten them up over the winter before shipping them to the slaughterhouses in Chicago. The cowboys who drove them a thousand miles north were a lusty lot who spent 16 hours a day in the saddle, choking on dust, watching out for marauding Indians, heading off stampedes and fighting rustlers and armed farmers who didn't like to see all those cows trampling their crops.

A trail drive averaged about 2,500 head of cattle which were driven an average of 1,500 miles. A trail boss, in charge of about a dozen cowboys and a cook, was completely responsible for the operation, and shared the profits once the cattle were sold. His cowhands were paid about $30 a month and board.

Naturally, all that work made them thirsty. The cowtowns along the route obliged them with plenty to drink as well as friendly games of chance to help boost their income, and companionship to boost their morale. It was a tough life, often a short one, but to be a cowboy in the Wild West is still an American boy's fondest dream.

Cowboys, gunslingers and U.S. Marshals were only part of the population who tamed the Wild West, however. In 1862, President Lincoln signed a law that entitled any American citizen (or anyone who intended to become one) to 160 acres of land for nothing more than a small filing fee and a promise to live there and farm it for a least five years. Civil War veterans went by the thousands to Kansas and Nebraska, the Dakotas and Montana, to take the Government up on its offer. Europeans were lured by the promise of a free farm, too, and in less than a generation the country's population doubled. The cowboys called the homesteaders "Sodbusters." The law required them to be farmers, but the farms got in the way of the cattle drives. The Indians didn't like their fenced-in acres either, but they were clearly there to stay.

The cowboys and Indians had another enemy, too. Sheep herders. After the Spanish brought sheep to California, the Indians themselves helped spread herds into Colorado and Texas. By the time the "Sodbusters" began arriving, the "Woolies" had half a million head of sheep on the range and were at war with the cattle ranchers. One range war in Arizona lasted more than 5 years, and before it ended more than 30 men died. Up in Wyoming one night, masked men attacked four sheep camps, tied up the shepherds and clubbed 8,000 sheep to death.

In yet another scheme to encourage settlement of the West, the Government gave millions of acres of land to the railroads that were being built through the territory. The railroad companies mounted an advertising blitz telling Easterners, "You Need A Farm!" and thousands agreed. They carried their campaign into Europe, and Germans, Dutch, Swedes, Norwegians and Danes responded enthusiastically. In Minnesota and the Dakotas, the Scandinavian languages became more common than English.

So many people flowed into the West that the Government decided it was time to relocate the "Indian Territory." They forced the Creeks and Seminoles to sell some of their land and they called it "Oklahoma." On April 22, 1889, it was declared open under the Homestead Act, and before noon on that day almost 2 million acres had been claimed. Before the sun set, the cities of Guthrie and Oklahoma City had been established. Four years later, the Government bought out the Cherokee territory and 100,000 people moved in on the first day it was declared open.

Meanwhile, people were starving in Ireland; the political situation in Germany was driving people away, and in less than 30 years, beginning in 1831, 3,500,000 people from those two countries decided to become Americans. At the same time, another 1,500,000 migrated from other countries.

Between 1855 and 1890, more than 7 million arrived from Europe through New York alone! They kept coming for more than 60 years after that, and between 1890 and 1954, when the immigration laws were changed, 20 million people from just about every country in the world came to put their mark on America.

By 1872, it was apparent that expansion was dramatically changing the shape of the land. The mountain men wouldn't have recognized their lonely territory, and the old frontiers in Ohio and Tennessee were completely tamed. To preserve some of the natural beauty of the land, the Government set aside a tract of more than 3,470 square miles (an area bigger than the Commonwealth of Puerto Rico), in Wyoming, Montana and Idaho, and called it Yellowstone National Park. It's the oldest and still the biggest of the country's 37 National Parks. Yellowstone hasn't changed much since hunters, trappers and Indians roamed there more than 200 years ago. It's wild country with moose, elk and more, including a huge population of bears. The territory is laced with geysers and natural hot springs, some with temperatures as high as 200°F. The best known, Old Faithful, sends a jet of water and steam 200 feet into the air every 65 minutes, as regular as clockwork. It's as much a symbol of America to many people as the Statue of Liberty.

Yellowstone straddles the Continental Divide, a range of high mountains that separates East from West. Rivers from the east of it flow toward the Atlantic; from the west, water flows towards the Pacific. Further north in Montana, and spilling across the Canadian border, the Continental Divide is at its spectacular best in Glacier National Park. It's home to bighorn sheep and grizzly bears and snow that never melts. It was named for the glaciers that carved its breathtaking valleys, but there are still glaciers there, and it's as much like Alaska as any other spot in the lower 48 States.

Daniel Boone would still recognize the country's most-visited National Park, the Great Smoky Mountains in North

Carolina and Tennessee. He'd know the restored log buildings and split rail fences; he'd probably stop for a chat with the local blacksmith or pick up some corn meal at the gristmill. But he'd be a little surprised to find nature trails for cars. Actually, though, if he thought about it, he'd smile, to think that the majority of the 8 million people who tour the park every year never get out of their cars and that leaves the mountaintops and winding trails quiet and peaceful. It makes it possible to explore in the same way he did, and possibly not run into anyone else doing the same thing.

Americans are very attached to their cars and rarely go anywhere without them. The result is that many see America as superhighways carefully designed to carry traffic around the small towns and big cities, with interchanges full of ugly gas stations, tacky motels and fast food stands. Others in search of America fly over it in big jets and hope there are no clouds over the Grand Canyon to ruin the view.

It's a part of America that exists, there's no denying it. But there's another America out there. And it's worth exploring.

Way out West in the wilds of New Mexico, there's a roadside oasis that's a combination gas station, general store, restaurant, meat market and dance hall. On Friday nights, folks drop in for a little companionship, a little gossip, a little something to eat and a few beers. Some of them travel as far as 100 miles for the pleasure, because people are few and far between out there. The population is 0.3 persons per square mile, in fact.

The Friday night get-togethers are repeated in dozens of places along the old cattle driving routes. They were generally spaced about a day's drive apart and usually boasted a well. Today they pump gas instead of water and their customers arrive in pickup trucks rather than on horseback. But they bring the spirit of the West along with them. It's here that they buy all their gas and most of their food. And when they feel like a night on the town, they drop around for a T-bone steak and salad. They buy toys for their kids and batteries for their trucks. They go to make phone calls, because many never bothered to install phones at home. And if the Friday night party lasts too long, they stay the night in the attached motel.

In one of them on a Friday night not too long ago a woodcutter, who said he worked from six in the morning until sundown, seven days a week, summed up what it's all about:

"When you're working that hard, that late, that long, you sure do appreciate a place like this to come and have a beer and relax," he said. And why does he work "that late, that long?" "Sometimes I hate to come in," he added, "it gets so pretty out there it hurts your eyes."

Up among the cornfields in the Midwest, the rhythm of life is a little different. People live in small towns with populations of five or six hundred on tree-shaded streets that criss-cross a main road where the stores are located. In most of them, the supper hour is announced at six in the evening with a blast from the siren on top of the firehouse. An hour later, the younger children drift downtown for an ice cream cone. They hang around for a while, but eventually they're replaced by teenagers out for a Coke and some companionship. They arrive on motorbikes or in souped-up cars with the rear-ends high in the air and the radios turned up even higher. When they get tired of the pinball games at the local drive-in, they drive up and down the quiet streets impressing the girls on the sidewalk by "peeling rubber" as they take off from a traffic light. It doesn't take them long to get bored with all that fun, and they soon settle down for a serious discussion about the high school football team; about girls, if they're boys, or about boys, if they're girls. By 11, the town has shut down for the night, and the only sounds are from crickets or a truck just passing through.

While their kids are enjoying themselves downtown, their parents are probably sitting out on the front porch, talking softly with a neighbor, listening to the sounds of the night, or complaining about all the racket those youngsters are making with their cars. Some nights they go downtown themselves. Down to the Elks or the Moose or the American Legion clubhouse. In many small towns in the middle of America, the fraternal organizations are at the center of the social life. They promote Americanism, the old values, neighborliness. And they provide a place to have a friendly drink and good coversation. They might sponsor bingo games for the ladies, poker parties for their husbands and buffet dinners for the whole family. On Saturday night, they pull out all the stops and turn the lodge hall into a dance hall where folks can take a turn to the music of Glenn Miller or Lawrence Welk, or swing and sway with Sammy Kaye.

Down in Georgia and Alabama and other parts of the Old South, community life is more often centered around the churches. One of the lures of the fraternal orders has always been to provide a place where an upstanding businessman could have a relaxing stinger or a grasshopper without running the risk of losing customers who might see him leaving the local saloon. In many parts of the South "Temperance" is too important a virtue for businessmen or politicians to unwind anywhere but behind the closed doors of their own homes.

The Southern churches, usually Methodist or Baptist, claim to give them all the unwinding they need, with singing and praying and inspiring preaching. Everybody goes to Sunday school, and the church supper is an event no one ever misses. To get ready for one, the ladies prepare casseroles, cakes, puddings, fried chicken, hams and biscuits. When it all comes together, it's one of life's great pleasures. These Southern Protestants deny themselves one of the things other Americans consider a pleasure: dancing. Not long ago a preacher in Knoxville, Tennessee, explained it to his parish by telling them: "Any man who says he can dance and keep his thoughts pure is less than a man or he is a liar!" The congregation, as they often do, answered him with a chorus of "Amens."

Sometimes Americans seek their pleasure by traveling abroad. But in their hearts, they know home's best. A woman in Dubuque, Iowa, explained how she felt: "It was wonderful to get back to the Old World charm of Dubuque. You know, the hills here are very reminiscent of Switzerland. And, oh, our river! Now, I've never seen anything, neither the Danube nor the Seine, that's as beautiful as the Mississippi."

A lot of them travel around the United States sharing the pleasures of other regions. They travel in mobile homes, in pickup trucks with little, house-like affairs set precariously in the back and up over the roof, and they travel in cars. For those in cars who aren't packing their own sleeping quarters, there are more than 55,000 motels waiting to serve them, and a decade ago, Holiday Inns reported that they were adding a new motel to the landscape every 72 hours!

In quieter times, when there were no Interstate Highways and cars didn't go over 30, people stayed overnight as paying guests in private houses that called themselves "tourist homes."

A lot of them still exist in small towns all across the country, but since the network of concrete spaghetti they call "super" highways take tourists over and around the small towns, tourists homes are being starved out, even though they charge about half as much as the fancy motels. A typical tourist home might be a big, old Victorian house on a town's main street; the yard studded with bright orange daylilies, the lawn shaded by tall, old trees. The proprietors are often a retired couple living otherwise on a Social Security pension, and you can find them relaxing on the wide porch in front of the house. The rooms set aside for the "paying guests" are scrupulously clean and simply furnished. The twin beds may have been bought as surplus from a local hospital, and are probably the most comfortable anyone ever slept in. And sometimes, for a pittance of an extra charge, a tourist can begin the new day with a home-cooked breakfast. It's a slice of life left over from the 1930s, and though many people claim to long for those times when life was slower and people seemed friendlier, they blithely pass it by, leaving it to die.

The old ways are alive and well in many parts of the country, though. In New England clambakes, in Louisiana crawfish festivals, Oklahoma rodeos and Iowa tractor-pulling contests. Traditions like the Memorial Day parade, the Fourth of July picnic, Little League baseball and Sunday afternoon softball games bind us all to each other as well as to the past. High school football, band concerts and senior proms give us a sense of community. The beauty and abundance of the land itself gives us a sense of pride.

Express passenger trains don't roar across the plains any more. Hillbillies have been transplanted to "Deetroit City" from the mountains of West Virginia. And a lot of the cotton fields down South are producing soybeans these days. But they still ride to hounds on the Eastern Shore in Maryland. They still play sweet Dixieland music in New Orleans. They still make Bourbon from good Kentucky corn and produce more beer than any other nation on earth.

Dodge City, Kansas, "the wickedest little city in the world" in Bat Masterson's day, is a little bit bigger and a whole lot less wicked these days. It's a tidy, prosperous city, home to 17,000 people who make farm machinery and drum heads and fatten cattle on their way to market. They also run a thriving business catering to tourists who are dying to see the cemetery up on Boot Hill. The women who live there these days are more likely to be dressed in blue jeans than calico. And none of the men carries a six-gun any more.

Blue jeans, like jazz and corn on the cob, are America's gift to the world. But more important is America's spirit and enthusiasm, a thing they call "The American Dream."

From the first day the first settler arrived from Europe, Americans have been excited about the idea that anything is possible. You can start from nothing and *be* somebody. You can control your own destiny, realize your wildest dream; or even be free *not* to be a superachiever if that's what your dream is all about.

Back in 1959, Nikita Khruschev toured the United States from New York to Coon Rapids, Iowa to Hollywood, California. When he arrived in movieland he was given the red carpet treatment in a tour of the studios of 20th Century Fox, guided by no less a person than Spiros Skouras, the president of the company.

That evening at dinner, Skouras, one of the great movie czars of all time, explained to the Russian Premier that he had originally arrived in the United States as a penniless immigrant from Greece. "Only in America," he said, "could a young man with such humble beginnings make it straight to the top."

"I understand that very well", answered Khruschev. "My father was a coal miner in Soviet Georgia."

Putdowns notwithstanding, the American Dream works. At the last count, more than half a million Americans, a quarter of one percent of the population, reported a net worth of over a million dollars. Most of them live in New York and California, and Texas ranks tenth in millionaire population after Indiana, Idaho and Minnesota.

And every year, thousands of immigrants still renounce foreign princes and potentates in an oath that makes them American citizens. The busiest naturalization center in the country is, appropriately, in Brooklyn, New York. Some 30,000 take the oath there every year in a courtroom decorated with original murals from the now-closed immigration center on Ellis Island in New York Harbor.

The murals show laborers working with picks and shovels, but the new citizens are more likely to be computer programmers than mine workers. Immigrants these days are more middle class, better educated and younger than the Irish, Italian and Middle European people who crowded through New York a generation ago.

They come from more diverse places, too. Not long ago, on a day 329 potential citizens arrived in that Brooklyn courtroom, the majority, 49 of them, came from Jamaica. The rest were from 55 different countries, including one Russian, and a Greek who had written a song that had been a hit in America ten years before.

The judge who administered the oath is himself the son of an Italian immigrant and has been naturalizing foreign-born citizens for two decades. The process takes about three hours, including a literacy test, which these days about 95 percent of the applicants pass easily. Some of them change their names along with their nationality, like Harry Gerolymatos, who decided to Americanize himself to Harris Gerolymatos!

And why do they go to the trouble? A Pakistani immigrant explained: "I decided it is better to be a citizen of the country, the people of which reached the moon. Even if I do not reach the moon, I want to be among the people who reached the moon."

Once having taken the oath, nothing at all distinguishes them from all the other American citizens. They move on to places like Moscow, Pa, Cairo, Ga, Bagdad, Arizona or Paradise, Michigan.

Some might go to Canton, Ill., which was named for Canton, China, which the original settlers were sure would be reached if you dug a deep enough hole. Or out to West Texas, where a cowboy once said, "You can lie on your belly and see for miles. Of course, there ain't nothing to see, but if there was, you could see it."

They could send their children to a one-room schoolhouse in Nebraska. They could get a job in a monster shopping mall just about anywhere. They can do just about anything they want. Anything, that is, except run for President. But as native-born Americans, their children can become President, possibly even their girl-children.

And that, above all, is what the American Dream is all about.

Facing page: Waimea Canyon, Hawaii.

Above: ranchland on the Hamakua Coast, whose rugged cliffs (facing page) are carpeted with lush, subtropical vegetation. Overleaf: (left) the dark sand of many of Hawaii's beaches testifies to the volcanic forces that have created such spectacular scenery. Right: a waterfall cascades into the depths of the Hona Kane Iki Valley.

In 1829, as part of their rejection of the old gods, Christian Hawaiians destroyed the City of Refuge, or Pu'uhonua (these pages). It has since been rebuilt and restored to its former charm and is now the showpiece of a National Historic Park.

The island of Oahu (these pages and overleaf) is the site of Hawaii's capital, Honolulu, known as "The Gathering Place." Although heavily populated, Oahu still boasts the lush, dramatic countryside and glorious surf-fringed beaches, as at Sunset Beach (above), that have become synonymous with the state. Facing page and overleaf right: the Koolau Range is the remains of the two volcanic domes which formed the island. Overleaf left: the Pali coast.

25

Above: Alaska's famous 800-mile-long pipeline, which carries oil from the Prudhoe Bay field to the Valdez terminal. In 1980, Mount McKinley National Park was renamed Denali National Park (facing page and overleaf), though its focal point is still the mighty Mount McKinley, North America's highest mountain, whose face is continuously carved and shattered by the Ruth Glacier (overleaf left). Overleaf right: the Nenana River.

A familiar and charming sight in Alaska is the caribou (above), one of the commonest members of the deer family in the state. Facing page: the spectacular Mat-Su Valley. Overleaf: the 4,000 square-mile Juneau Icefield, which feeds the Mendenhall Glacier (left). This extraordinary, creeping river of ice has become, along with the 20,320 feet high Mount McKinley (right), one of Alaska's major tourist attractions.

Alaska's famous Iditarod Trail Race is a 1,049-mile dogsled marathon run annually, from Anchorage to Nome. Vicious, freezing gales, as at Shaktoolik (facing page), and seemingly endless stretches of pack ice (above) are just two of the many trials the competitors and their teams must endure.

Previous pages: the volcanic tendencies of the Pacific Northwest were brought violently to notice when Washington's Mount St. Helens (left) erupted on May 18, 1980, devasting over 150 square miles of forest. Oswald West, the Governor of Oregon from 1911 to 1915, was keen to preserve the beauty of Oregon's coastline for posterity, thus, there are many state-protected areas, such as Samuel Boardman State Park (right). Facing page: looking south from Ecola State Park. Above: Crater Lake, in southeast Oregon, is almost 2,000 feet deep and has no outlet or inlet. Due, however, to perfectly balanced evaporation and rainfall, the water level hardly varies.

Warm Springs River (previous pages left) and spectacular Sahalie Falls (previous pages right) hint at the splendor and diversity of the Oregon countryside. Above: icicles pull down the already snow-laden branches of trees at Crater Lake Lodge. Facing page: an army of rocks seems to march from the sea on to Harris Beach State Park.

Above: a golden grain field and (facing page) sunbaked grazing land, near Yuba City, in California. Overleaf: (left) a view of the coast from the Klamath Overlook and (right) Ladybird Johnson Grove of coast redwoods, one of many breathtaking natural wonders in California.

The snowy peak of Mount Shasta (these pages) seems to belong to a different world from that of the sunny countryside 14,000 feet below. Overleaf: (left) Burnley Falls, east of Enterprise, spill over the rocks in delicate threads of water, and (right) near Sacramento, a vessel glides along a waterway that is bordered by a patchwork pattern of richly colored fields.

51

In Lassen Volcanic National Park, the steaming springs and boiling mud pools of Bumpass Hell (these pages) bear witness to the area's volcanic and thermal activity. Overleaf: (left) a cable car ascends Eagles Nest, which affords a spectacular view of Lake Tahoe, and (right) a sternwheeler glides through the placid waters of Emerald Bay, Emerald Bay.

With the arrival of spring, the Dana River (above) becomes a gushing torrent of melted snow. Facing page: vacationers relax in the stillness and silence of Silver Lake, in the High Sierras. Overleaf: Yosemite National Park is a place of astounding natural beauty, with such sights as (left) the cascading Vernal Falls and (right) Half Dome, transformed into a magical, burnished mass as it reflects the golden glow of sunset.

Previous pages: (right) the Upper and Lower Yosemite Falls, in Yosemite National Park, and (left) the huge sequoias which are the showpiece of Kings Canyon National Park, east of Fresno. At Monterey (above) the Californian coastline has a rocky, rugged charm. Facing page: the Bixby Creek Bridge links the walls of a chasm in a graceful arc, 260 feet above the water.

Previous pages: (right) the jagged peninsula of Point Lobos and (left) a sand sculpture crafted by the sea at Point Lobos State Reserve, which is well known for the proliferation of Monterey cypresses. Above: farmland near Livermore, east of San Francisco. Point Reyes Lighthouse (facing page), stands on a lonely, desolate crag, commanding fine views of the treacherously-rocky coast north of San Francisco.

Previous pages: now a State Historic Park, Bodie (left), is a decayed reminder of a once booming gold mining town that in the mid-nineteenth century supported 65 saloons and averaged one murder each day, and (right) cacti in Anza-Borrego Desert State Park. Above: on the border between Nevada and Arizona, the Colorado River meets the Hoover Dam to form one of the world's largest man-made lakes, Lake Mead, which measures 227 square miles. Facing page and overleaf: farmland south-west of Boise, Idaho.

Montana's Glacier National Park contains fifty glaciers, two hundred sparkling lakes, and many other sights at which to marvel, such as (above) the view from Logan Pass, (facing page) a healthy crop of glacier lilies, with Mount Clements beyond, (overleaf right) the sheer face of Garden Wall towering over McDonald Creek, and (overleaf left) Swiftcurrent Lake, with the symmetrical form of Grinnell Point and Gould Mountain on the horizon.

In Wyoming, the Rockies offer scenery of breathtaking beauty in the form of the serrated, blue-gray peaks of the Grand Tetons (these pages and overleaf), which came under the protection of Grand Teton National Park in 1929. These striking mountains soar for over a mile above diverse landscapes, including (overleaf right) the Shoshone River, which provides an exciting raft trip and (overleaf left) the tranquil Jenny Lake.

Over a hundred years ago, the awe-inspiring beauty of Yellowstone moved a few far-sighted men to establish the world's first national park here. Apart from spectacular mountain scenery, such as Mount Moran (above) mirrored in Oxbow Bend, Yellowstone has blue, coiling rivers (overleaf left) and dense pine forests (overleaf right) teeming with wildlife. Facing page: the Snake River winds its way through Grand Teton National Park.

Among Yellowstone's many attractions are a number of active hot springs and geysers, such as Castle Geyser (above). Facing page: Grand Teton itself, is the highest peak in the Grand Teton range.

The vast, barren expanse of Capitol Reef National Park in Utah is enhanced by the marvelous shades and tints of the sandstone that is carved into strange, beautiful shapes, such as Hickman Natural Bridge (above). Facing page: striking sandstone sculptures are also found in Monument Valley, on the Utah/Arizona border. Canyonland's National Park in Utah (overleaf) exhibits some of the most incredible examples of water erosion, such as that of the Colorado River (left) and of its tributary the Green River (right).

Behind Glen Canyon Dam, the Colorado River has swollen to form the 186-mile-long Lake Powell (above), which, with its canyon-indented shoreline, forms the Glen Canyon National Recreation Area. Facing page: unbroken blue sky creates a backdrop for the startling rock formations of Monument Valley.

The play of light and shadow on Arizona's Monument Valley (above) heightens the drama of the landscape. Apart from beauty, the canyons also contain interesting history: Canyon De Chelly (facing page) exhibits evidence of ive Indian cultures. Overleaf pages: the subtle, pink-orange hues of the Grand Canyon.

Previous pages: (left) Monument Valley's East and West Mittens silhouetted against the sunset sky and (right) Canyon de Chelly, which is still cultivated by the Navajo Indians. Above: sunset turns the Grand Canyon at Yaki Point into shifting patterns of muted color and golden light. Facing page: looking from Mather Point on the East Rim Drive, a view of the horizon reveals the uniform height of the Grand Canyon's rim.

Previous pages: (left) tall saguaro cacti break up a horizon of barren hills in Saguaro National Monument and (right), Arizona Biltmore Resort, where a lush, green golf course is edged with luxury residences commanding fine views of the Camelback Mountains. In Colorado, the Central Rockies seem to make a desperate effort to reach the sky, rising sharply from the Great Plains to form snow-covered mountains of great beauty. Above: the Berthoud Pass, just west of Denver, affords views of the Arahapo National Forest. The slopes of Vail (facing page) comprise North America's largest single mountain ski resort.

Previous pages: (left) the Loveland Pass and (right) Telluride, both in Colorado. Facing page: a chair lift takes skiers up the face of Aspen Mountain, Colorado. Above: the buildings of Steamboat Springs. Overleaf: (left) a graceful bridge carries Highway 24 across a valley near Redcliff and (right) the dramatic Red Rocks, near Denver.

Above: skiers from Steamboat Springs prepare for a run on Thunderhead. Facing page: red and yellow gondolas climb into the snow-covered hills around Vail. Overleaf: (left) the brightly-colored houses of Telluride and (right) the forested slopes around Steamboat.

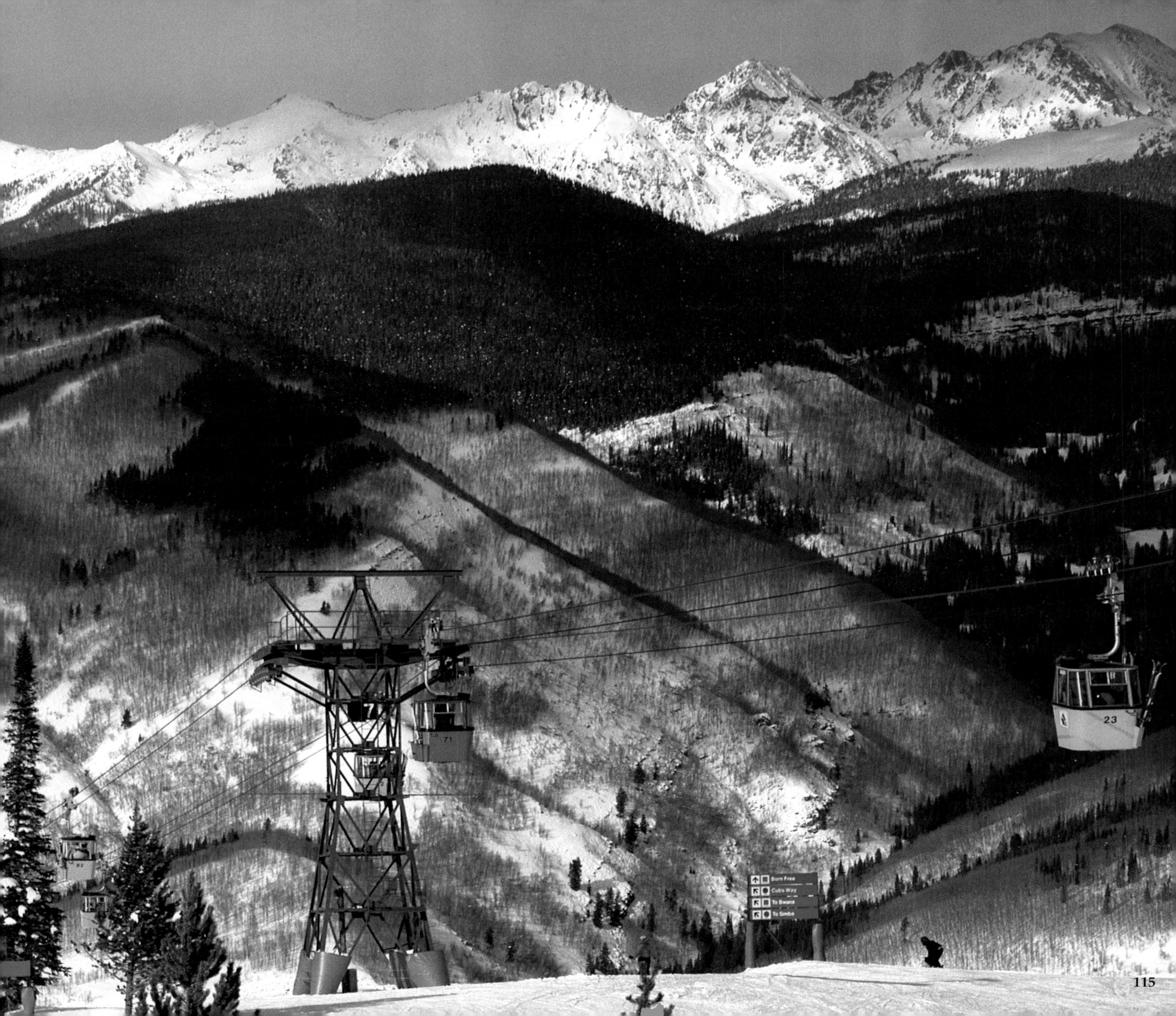
Born Free
Cubs Way
23

The forests, lakes and streams, released from the icy grip of winter, form some of the loveliest and most dramatic scenes of Colorado's summer. Above: dark-green conifers sweep down to the shores of Bear Lake, in Rocky Mountain National Park. Facing page: the Uncompahgre River in the San Juan Gorge, near Ouray. Overleaf: aspen and conifer covered slopes in Gunnison National Forest.

Above: the tumbledown structure of Lost Horse Mill, near the ghost town of Crystal, Colorado. Facing page: fall brings a rich, golden color to the aspens of Colorado.

Above: the crumbling remains of Fort Union, New Mexico, which protected the Santa Fe Trail between 1851 and 1891. Facing page: the spectacular interior of Carlsbad Caverns, beneath the Guadalupe Mountains. Overleaf: (left) sunset silhouettes the masts of yachts in Corpus Christi Harbor, and (right) farmland near Hereford, both in Texas.

Above: a farm in a neatly plowed field south of Corpus Christi. Facing page: Palo Duro Canyon, near Amarillo.
Overleaf: (left) an oil refinery on Navigation Boulevard, Corpus Christi, and (right) feed lots at Hereford, where beef cattle are fattened up for sale.

Oklahoma has come a long way since the dark days of the dustbowl, when much of the state's farmland simply blew away. Careful conservation programs and irrigation techniques have returned the fertility to the soil, as the land around Oklahoma City (these pages) reveals.

The huge grain fields of Kansas (overleaf), which yield hundreds of millions of bushels of wheat a year, are the basis of the state's prosperity, and much of the population is employed in growing or processing it. The state has other sights to draw the tourist, however, such as the Chalk Pyramids (facing page) at Monument Rocks, south of Oakley, and the golf course (above) near Wichita.

The Cornhusker State of Nebraska has always been thought of as a rich land of gentle gradients, and that is just what most of it is – (above) Highway 83 leading north into North Platte and (facing page) scenes west of Ogallala – but dramatic scenery can be found at Chimney Rock (overleaf left) and (overleaf right) Scots Bluff National Monument.

Just above Pierre, the Missouri River is blocked by the Oahe Dam, creating Lake Oahe (these pages). Overleaf: (left) River Valley Cedar Pass in Badlands National Park and (right) the Wagon Train Compound in South Dakota's Custer State Park.

Previous pages: sheer rock walls in Badlands National Park. Above: a deserted farm building and (facing page) freshly gathered bales of hay in Walworth County, South Dakota. Overleaf: (left) an oil well near Tioga and (right) a church near Williston, both in North Dakota.

Facing page: irrigation on farmland east of Williston. Above: the restored blockhouses of Fort Abraham Lincoln, from which Custer marched out to his death in 1876. Today, costumed staff and authentic equipment recreate the atmosphere of fort life in the days of the fatal campaign. Overleaf: (left) the wooded shoreline of Lake Superior and (right) the lighthouse at Grand Marais, both in Minnesota.

Facing page: Split Rock Lighthouse, which is the tallest lighthouse in the nation and now serves as the focus of a Minnesota state park. Above: a creek near Split Rock. Overleaf: (left) tumbling waters on the Gooseberry River and (right) foam on the Baptism River, both in Minnesota.

The waterways of Minnesota are among the loveliest in the nation, drawing many visitors to the state: (previous pages left) the Gooseberry River; (previous pages right) the Baptism River; (facing page) Leech Lake and (above) Rainy Lake, in Voyageurs National Park. Overleaf: (left) a road near Eau Claire, and (right) the small town of Bayfield, on Lake Superior, which offers regular trips to the Apostle Islands, both in Wisconsin.

The extreme northern edge of Wisconsin touches Lake Superior, giving the state a shoreline of startling beauty. During the winter the fresh water of the lake freezes easily, creating magical scenes, such as those around Port Wing (these pages).

Divided into two peninsulas and touched by four of the Great Lakes, Michigan is dominated by water. Above:
Lake Superior at Munising. Facing page: a barn on the Door Peninsula, Wisconsin. Overleaf: (left) the Coast
Guard Station at Marquette, on Lake Superior and (right) the pier and lighthouse at Grand Haven.

Previous pages: two very different bridges in Ohio: (left) a timber structure at Seven Caves, near Bainbridge, and (right) a steel structure over the Ohio at the Banks of Merieth. These pages: farm buildings and rich, productive land in Crawford County, Iowa, a predominantly agricultural region. Overleaf: (left) Alley Springs Mill and (right) Dillard Mill, both in Missouri.

Above: mist rises from the still surface of Lake Dardanelle while (facing page) tumbling waters spill from a smaller pond in Buffalo River State Park, Arkansas. Overleaf: two very different faces of Coahoma County, Mississippi: (left) a cotton harvesting machine and (right) cypress swamp.

Previous pages: (left) cypress trees in Cypress Gardens, near Winter Haven, and (right) great egrets and a wood stork in Corkscrew Swamp. Facing page: Cape Florida Lighthouse, one of the state's oldest buildings. Above: sunset over Key West, one of the most famous Florida islands.

Facing page: Okefenokee Swamp, a 600-square-mile swamp which straddles the Georgia-Florida border. Above: Westville, in Lumpkin, where several antebellum buildings are preserved. Overleaf: (left) the massive bulk of Atlanta's Stone Mountain, which boasts a 90-foot-high carving of Civil War figures, and (right) a gushing brook in Amicalola Falls State Park.

Above: a motorboat speeds across the still waters of Laura S. Walker State Park, near Okefenokee Swamp. Facing page: heavily-buttressed trees grow from a swamp near Tifton.

These pages: the neatly-laid-out paddocks and trim, red and white buildings of South Carolina's Cougham Farms, an extensive horse farm 15 miles east of Columbia. Overleaf: (left) a farm near the airport at Raleigh, capital of North Carolina, and (right) low cloud creeps between the peaks of Great Smoky Mountains National Park.

Above: cattle graze on rich pastureland in the Great Smoky Mountains. Facing page: the dramatic and spectacular Hanging Rock, with its equally impressive view of the forests around Danbury. Overleaf: (left) the Burgess Falls, near Murfreesboro, and (right) the Waynesboro Natural Bridge, Tennessee.

Previous pages: (left) the tranquil waters of Pickwick Landing and (right) the sheer drop of Falls Creek Falls. Above: the reconstructed Fort Loudon at Vonore, which was originally built in 1756. Facing page: the veil of water of the Burgess Falls, near Smyrna.

Facing page: a view from the Newfound Gap Road and (above) from the Little River Road, both in Great Smoky Mountains National Park. Overleaf: (left) the Old Mill at Pigeon Forge, which has been grinding grain since at least 1860, and (right) a gentle sunset at Pickwick Landing.

Above: the bridge across the Tennessee at Paris Landing. Facing page: the Gregg-Cable House at Cades Cove, an isolated rural village whose quaint old buildings are now included in Great Smoky Mountains National Park.

The ability of Kentucky's bluegrass to produce fine livestock is legendary, and its abundance is shown (above) near Frankfort, (facing page) Almahurst Farm, near Lexington, and (overleaf left) near Lexington. Overleaf right: the golden light of sunset silhouettes bridges across the Ohio at Louisville.

Previous pages: the waters along the Chincoteague waterfront, Virginia, (right) and the brilliant colors of a West Virginian fall landscape (left). Facing page: the tobacco house at the Booker T. Washington National Monument. Above: cattle gazing at Appomattox Court House National Historic Park. Overleaf: (left) Humpback Bridge near Covington, the oldest and most famous covered bridge in Virginia, and (right) the New Cape Henry Light, the tallest cast-iron lighthouse in the nation.

Facing page: a farm near Farmington, Delaware. Above: the impressive engineering feat of the Bay Bridge across Chesapeake Bay, Maryland.

Though often thought of as an industrial state, much of New Jersey is surprisingly rural in character, (these pages) horses at the Bar-M Ranch Training Center near Sparta. Overleaf: (left) a waterfall at Lafayette, in northern New Jersey, and (right) large merchant ships off the New Jersey coast.

Previous pages: (left) the gleaming tracks of the Black River and Western Railway and (right) Spring Lake. Above: the broad beach of Cape May, one of the oldest and loveliest seaside resorts in the nation. Facing page: a wooden pier at Wildwood. Overleaf: (left) a metal bridge crosses the Raritan River near Bunnvale, and (right) Leamings Run Botanical Gardens at Swainton.

These pages and overleaf: scenes from Pennsylvania's Lancaster County, where the strong Amish community maintains age-old farming techniques and ways of life as part of their religion.

232

Previous pages: (left) a wooden walkway at Bushkin Falls, Pennsylvania, which were opened to the public in 1904, and (right) the 50-mile chasm of Pine Creek, known as the Grand Canyon of Pennsylvania. These pages: farmland in Amish country.

Above: Fire Island Lighthouse on Long Island, New York State, with the resort of Kismet beyond. Facing page: Asharoken and boats moored in Northport Bay, (overleaf left) islands in Great South Bay and (overleaf right) Montauk Lighthouse, all on Long Island.

Previous pages: the changing seasons bring different colors to The Mall, in New York's Central Park. Facing page: Crab Meadow Park and Golf Course near Northport. Above: looking east over Southold, on Long Island. Overleaf: the tumbling waters gush over the rim of Niagara Falls.

Above: the city of Hartford, the largest in Connecticut, with its cathedral in the foreground. Facing page and overleaf right: Mystic Seaport at Mystic, a carefully restored seafaring port of the last century. Overleaf left: the Harkness Memorial State Park near Goshen Point, with its 42-room mansion and 200 acres of grounds.

Previous pages left: some of the magnificent houses which were built on the hills above Newport, Rhode Island, by the rich and famous towards the end of last century. Previous pages right and these pages: the magnificent Newport Bridge, which spans the waters of Narragansett Bay.

Above: the Highland Light of 1797, the oldest of the many lighthouses along Massachusetts' Cape Cod peninsula.
Facing page: the rugged scenery of Gay Head Cliffs, on Martha's Vineyard. Overleaf: (left) sand dunes at
Provincetown and (right) the snow-covered beach at Duxbury.

Above: West Falmouth, on the southwestern coast of Cape Cod. Facing page: Menemsha Harbor, Martha's Vineyard.
Overleaf: (left) Cobb's Pond and the beach stretching between West Brewster and East Brewster, and (right) low
tide near Brewster.

Above: a motor boat disturbs the sparkling waters of Westport. Facing page: the 250-foot-tall Pilgrim Monument at Provincetown, which commemorates the first landing of the Pilgrim Fathers in 1620. Overleaf: (left) Vermont's Winooski River, near Waterbury, and (right) a covered bridge near Waterville Village.

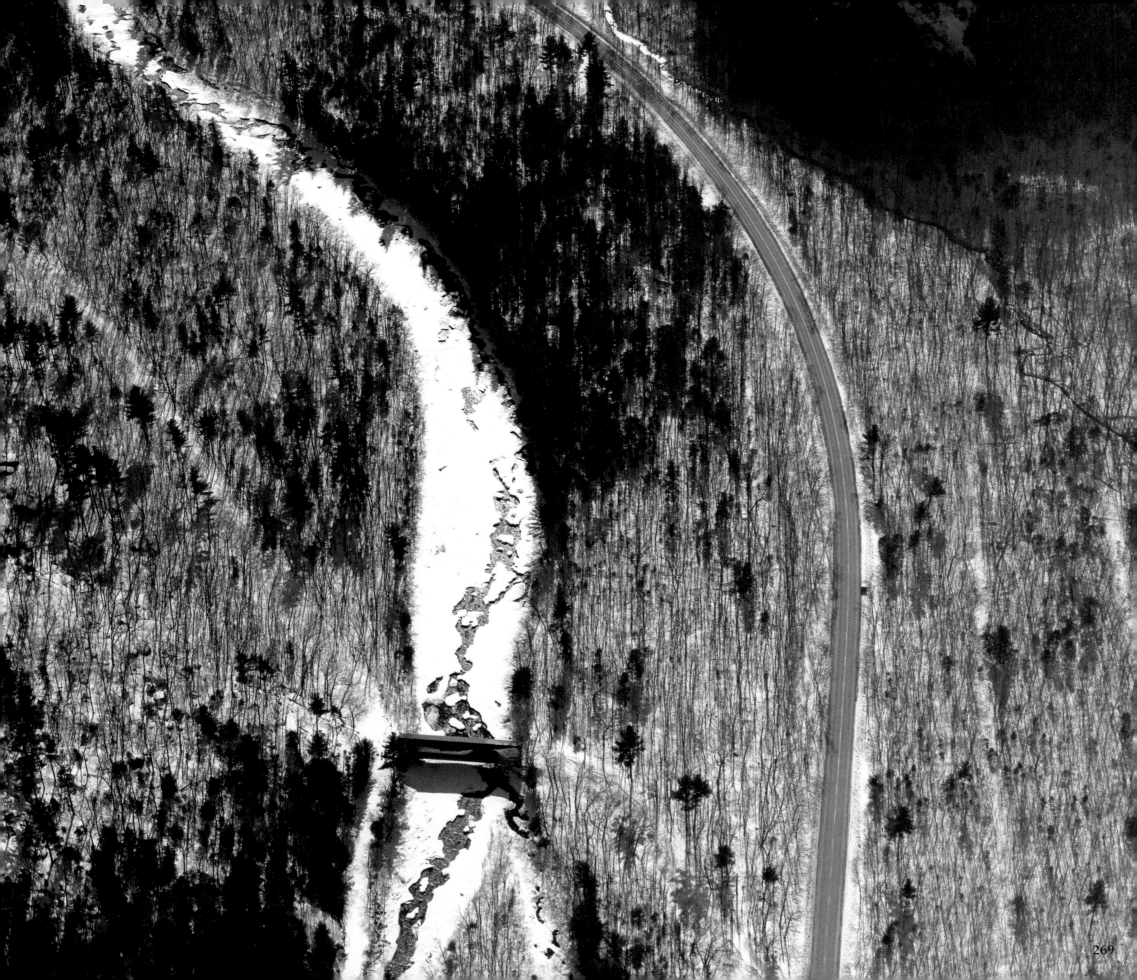

269

Above: forests, agricultural land and farm buildings near Morrisville, Vermont. Facing page: the rural town of Hyde Park. Overleaf: (left) the Winooski River, near Waterbury, and (right) mist envelops nearby snow-covered fields.

Previous pages: (left) an icy river near Rutland, Vermont, and (right) the Middlebury River at Ripton. Facing page: brightly-colored farm buildings near Rutland and (above) a plainer nearby rural scene.

Fall brings great beauty to the forests of New Hampshire. Facing page: the slopes of Ellis River Valley, White Mountain National Forest. Above: Echo Lake, near Conway. Overleaf: (left) a scene beside the Kancamagus Highway in White Mountain National Forest and (right) Whitneys Inn, Jackson.

Above: the snow-covered summit of Mount Washington, New Hampshire. Facing page: skiers at the skiing resort of Bretton Woods. Overleaf: (left) a woodland home at Jackson, and (right) the Union Church of 1853 and covered bridge at Stark.

Previous pages: (left) the beautifully-sited Mount Washington Hotel and (right) the carefully-tended slopes of
Waterville Valley Ski Resort. Above: the Washington Valley from Sugar Hill. Facing page: the Lower Falls of
the Swift River in the Rocky Gorge Scenic Area. Overleaf: (left) the Glen Ellis Falls and (right) a scene near
the Kancamagus Highway, both in the White Mountain National Forest.

Above: the tumbling waters of the aptly-named Swift River, White Mountain National Forest. Facing page: mist and low cloud swirls along the Washington Valley near North Conway. Overleaf: (left) the small fishing town of Port Clyde and (right) Cape Elizabeth Lighthouse, near Portland, both in Maine.

Above: sunrise on Mount Cadillac. Facing page: Bucksport, where during a border dispute with Britain, a fort was built in 1846. Overleaf: (left) yachts moored in a secure Maine bay and (right) Stonington, a center for Maine's celebrated seafood cuisine.

Above: a small dinghy sails into the fishing harbor of Port Clyde. Facing page: Bass Harbor Light, on Mount Desert Island. Overleaf: (left) West Quoddy Head Lighthouse and (right) small craft in Stonington Harbor.

INDEX